FIVE WISDOMS
FOR
ENTREPRENEUR
SURVIVAL

FIVE WISDOMS FOR ENTREPRENEUR SURVIVAL

Practical Experience & Biblical Perspective

Todd Hopkins

JSM Publishing

FIVE WISDOMS FOR ENTREPRENEUR SURVIVAL

Printed in the United States of America

Published by
JSM Publishing
170 North Jackson Street
Franklin, IN 46131
U.S.A.
(317) 738-9280

ISBN: 0-9746671-0-2

Paperback, 2003

Scripture quotations marked (NIV) are taken from the Holy Bible:
New International Version.

This book is available for bulk purchases.
For information, call 1-317-738-9280.
Or email the author to todd@officepride.com

First Edition

10 9 8 7 6 5 4 3 2

Dedication

To my wife: *Michelle*

Thanks for being my best friend
and for making life
more fun every day.
I love you!

To my sons: *James, Sam* and *Matt*

I am blessed to be
your Dad.
You guys are Awesome!

Table of Contents

Contents

Contents

Introduction
Most People Who Start a Business Give up Too Soon

It happens one day while you are on vacation, doing your workout routine, or taking the dog for a walk. Something you hear or read or see transforms itself into an idea that takes shape in your mind. Without a grand announcement, the seed for your new business takes its first root. The idea turns into an exciting vision. You see success on the horizon and you are ready to reach for it. You will be your own boss so you will naturally work less, earn more and finally get the respect you deserve.

Things start to come together. You are in business! You walk tall and proud. You made it. You are an entrepreneur. But there is more! Sooner or later disaster strikes. With thunderbolt speed, costs start to rise and sales drop. You are working more and making less. Or maybe not working much at all. You don't want to pick up the phone anymore. Actually, you don't even feel like getting out of bed. Maybe this business was doomed from the start, you reason. It's not me, it's the market, the timing, the competition. If only you had known this before you even got started. And that is how it ends. You cut your losses. You get out. An entrepreneur no more, you find a safe place to lick your wounds. It wasn't for you.

What happened to the dream, the vision, and the excitement that would get you out of bed in the morning before the alarm went off? Consider this: You gave up too soon. Every day brought a new avalanche of challenges. There was nothing exciting in this flood of setbacks. In this blinding blizzard you lost sight of what propelled you into becoming an entrepreneur in the first place: your vision.

In this book, I share with you five priceless wisdoms for survival given to me by my mentor, plus a mixture of other practical experiences and Biblical perspectives on how to weather the storm that goes with being an entrepreneur.

Chapter One
Give it Up

They say that to have started is half the journey, but it also holds true that beginnings are sometimes shaky and uncertain. When I started Office Pride in 1992, I was excited and jumped in with both feet. I certainly had plenty of initiative and courage. Financially, everything was on the line. Six months later I faced the possibility that my infant business would not make it to adulthood. To me, this was a crisis!

The hardest thing about being in a crisis is to

Your word is a lamp to my

feet and a light for my path.

Psalm 119:105 (NIV)

Chapter Two
(Nugget One)
Pray for Favor & Wisdom

This was my mentor's first piece of advice:

"Do not pray for God to provide new clients. Pray for favor and wisdom from God instead. Wisdom to truly understand your prospective customers' needs, and favor that they will believe what you say and that they will hire you, and that you will be able to provide the service that you have promised."

5

Now let me tell you about my frame of mind when I received this advice. I had been paddling upstream for six months with shamefully meager results. I had relocated to a relatively small town where nobody knew me. I had called on every potential client I could think of in the larger Indianapolis area with no positive results. I had a wife at home expecting our first child. I was in a pressure cooker with the heat turned on high! My prayers were instinctively directed at what I thought I needed: customers! Please, please, please... if God would send me some customers then everything will fall into place. Richard's advice was enlightening. It broadened my field of vision, and it came at the precise moment I need-ed it most.

My prayer life became more focused on seek-ing God's favor and wisdom. As a result, I became more focused myself. I became efficient and pro-ductive in everything I was doing. I started to do far more listening than talking - as the saying goes, that's why God gave us two ears and only one mouth. Instead of struggling to maintain my self-confidence to succeed in business, I shifted my confidence to God and trusted His ability to answer my prayers. I was no longer carrying my burden alone.

Within weeks, contracts were being signed. From a monthly gross sales figure of $550, we jumped to $1,700 in November, and then $5,900 in December. By January we had surpassed $7,000 in monthly sales. Before long, we were at $70,000 per month and the rest is history. For the next ten years, Office Pride would have an average annual growth rate of 57%.

Do I have your attention now? I thought so. Keep reading to find out the other four nuggets of wisdom my mentor shared with me.

Chapter Three
(Nugget Two)

Get Your Name Out

After the positive results obtained from applying the first item of advice from my mentor, I was eager for more.

This is what the second nugget of wisdom contained:

"Get your name out. People need to know who you are and what services your company provides."

This one seemed pretty obvious to me. I had been doing this all along, or so I thought. When I began Office Pride I was intent on establishing a good reputation in Johnson County where I had relocated. As I pondered about this advice I reviewed my strategy so far. I had begun soliciting business in Franklin and the surrounding areas. I realized everybody knew each other in a community of that size, but nobody knew me. I called on everyone I could think of and then expanded my efforts to the larger Indianapolis area. And that is when I realized that the advice had a deeper meaning. It was not just to broadcast my message around to the community, but to also let people KNOW ME as a neighbor and local businessman. As a person.

One of the first things I did as a new business owner was join the local Chamber of Commerce. There were many formal benefits to being a member of the Chamber, but the benefit I remember the most was not mentioned on any of the membership brochures; namely the enormous boost of confidence I received from the Executive Director and from one of the board members, a successful local entrepreneur. The Executive Director was always there to encourage me, and the board member shared with me her own struggles from when she had started her business. Furthermore, she decided to hire us as the janitorial service for her office building and proceeded to prod other chamber members to hire Office Pride too, since we were a member of the Chamber and trying to be a good corporate citizen in the community.

Suddenly the meaning of Richard's words became clear. He wasn't talking about advertising. He was talking about good old fashioned business **networking**. A smile broke on my face as I saw the proverbial light at the end of the tunnel become a strong beam of sunshine. I got involved in every networking opportunity I could find.

Chapter Four
(Nugget Three)
Be Accountable

I work in an industry where establishing trust is critical. The only way I know to gain the goodwill of my customers and business associates is to be worthy of their trust and to hold myself accountable to high standards. The third of five items of advice that I received from my newfound mentor provided a practical tool to achieve this goal:

"Be accountable to another businessman for the way you use your time and resources."

My mentor even went a step further and volunteered to play this role himself. This is a man I had just recently met. He did not know if I was worth his efforts. He had selflessly offered his wisdom and now he was also offering his time.

He said he would call me every day to ask if I had done everything necessary to achieve my goals for the day. I did not take him literally, reasoning that his integrity would hardly suffer if he happened to miss his call one or two times. But here was a man who stood behind his word. He did, in fact, call me every single day without fail.

This advice reached me at a time when I was spending my days cold calling and my nights doing the cleaning for our customers and working on proposals for new prospects. The hours faded into a blur of activity that left me too exhausted to take stock of my day. Like a boxer going to his corner after each gong to receive the pointers from his trainer, I would look forward to the daily phone calls as the opportunity to reconcile what I had done versus what I had set out to do that day. Even further, just knowing that the call was coming often provided the source of extra energy I needed to get a job done. I respected Richard's dedication and appreciated his steadfastness during this delicate phase in the growth of Office Pride.

I found this practice so helpful that I continue it to this day. I have a designated group of people who hold me accountable for the various aspects of the business. I also have two men with whom I meet weekly who hold me accountable to being a man of integrity. The significant benefits of having fellow business associates uphold my accountability are hard to measure. It is by far the one earthly factor that exerts the most influence over my major business decisions.

Chapter Five
(Nugget Four)
Get in Front of the Decision Makers

I remember my first sales call. I took a deep breath and made the phone call. I introduced myself and the reason why I was calling. I set an appointment for the following day to stop by and tell the prospect about my business. I showed up at the agreed time and made my presentation, smartly dressed and making sure to remember every single one of the features of the service I was offering. The presentation went smoothly and I was done in ten minutes. My prospect listened attentively and politely throughout my recitation. I thought the whole thing was going pretty well indeed. Until, at the very end, an ice mantle descended on my enthusiasm with the words: "... check back with me in six months." Oh, what a disappointment. This was the first of many meetings that would end with words to the same effect. Initially, I had hoped that these people I was meeting with would convey my message up the line, and that it would eventually reach the person with the authority to sign on the dotted line. It simply did not happen. Invariably, these people were polite and receptive, but they were not making the transition from prospects into customers.

The fourth nugget of wisdom from Richard, my mentor, was to:

"Develop a system to reach the decision makers in your sales efforts, instead of the trash can."

The key to this statement is, of course, the word system. I looked back on what I had been doing so far and the pattern of responses that I was getting. I identified a few statements that were getting a warmer response. I defined the number of calls to be made each day. By the second week in November, I had a very productive and well rehearsed phone script that I followed step by step to get appointments with the decision makers. I followed my new rule and did not accept an appointment with anybody else. The decision maker would have to hear it from me directly. I did not rely on third persons to transmit my message. I became a well-oiled prospecting machine. My working day would not be done until I had covered at least the minimum number of calls. Most of the time I exceeded that number. I found that my time was spent far more effectively. Now, at every chance I had to make a presentation, I was sitting across from the person who had the authority to give me the business right then and there. The nature of my presentations also changed. I had to become sharper because I was not getting the "inert" kind of listening any longer. There were highly inquisitive participants on the other side of the table now. They asked demanding questions and in turn forced me to become more focused in my answers. More importantly, decision makers knew what their organization needed. They would tell me about services and features that they find helpful. This gave my business the opportunity to respond to those needs. It amazes me, to this day, how well it worked.

Chapter Six
(Nugget Five)
Don't be Afraid to go For It

Once I had worked out a system to reach the decision makers on my sales calls, I had a fighting chance to convert these prospects into customers. Now the challenge was how to overcome their objections, and address their needs, so that they would give Office Pride their business. This was the last of five nuggets of wisdom I received from my business mentor:

"You can't afford to wait six months to increase sales. You need their business now. Don't be afraid

to go for the close if you know you are able to meet your prospect's needs."

His words touched on a key issue. My prospects had no urgency in making a decision to hire my services. Most of them already had some kind of working situation, whether they were happy with their existing provider or not. They had other things on their minds, and selecting the janitorial service was not on their top list of priorities. In contrast, time was quickly running out for my business. Either I increased my sales or I would be faced with an ugly decision fairly soon. Therefore, the burden of time was entirely on my side. So how could I turn the tables and give the prospect a reason to make a prompt decision? Would I blow my chances to get the account if I pushed too hard?

I boldly revamped my entire sales approach. By now I had enough confidence in Richard to trust the wisdom behind his advice. During my meetings, instead of rattling off a list of features and benefits about my business, I started to ask a series of questions that allowed me to flow directly into a "close" opportunity. The answers (to the type of questions I was asking) resulted in the prospect describing what they wanted in a janitorial service and asking if Office Pride could do the job for a specific price. At that point it was up to me to say "yes" or "no." Soon after implementing this new approach I began to see positive results. Not only did I close on prospects immediately, but I was also able to recognize which customers were not for me. Their answers to my questions would reveal unrealistic expectations or an unwillingness to accept price levels with a reasonable profit margin. Identifying those "dead ends" in a timely manner allowed me to spend my time on the prospects that offered a real chance of success.

I give God the credit for sending a fellow businessman my way who expressed interest in me as a young entrepreneur. I am grateful to my mentor for the wisdom he shared with me in the most generous spirit of good-fellowship. I aspire to honor his example and share the lessons I have learned, hopefully helping other young entrepreneurs overcome the challenges of their chosen paths.

But, that's not all.

Getting the customers was only half the battle. Now, I had employees and was I in for an awakening. Then came the cash flow issues, trying to keep peace at home and just keeping my own confidence in check.

Survival took on a whole new meaning. In the following chapters, I will share with you the attitude and activity that was required for me to survive the "rat race" of starting a business, risking everything, fearing failure and keeping success in proper perspective.

Chapter Seven
Stick it Out

Where do you find the strength to overcome the daily rejections, failures and disappointments that come with starting a business? Let me first tell you that you will encounter many obstacles along the way. These obstacles are normal. They are part of the process of starting, growing and operating a business. Once you learn to expect the downturns, you will be ready for them. You will have braced yourself to withstand the fall. You will get up, dust yourself off and keep going. You will get tough. You will do whatever it takes to keep the wheels of your vision turning. Eat beans and bread. Skip those cappuccinos. You can make that pair of shoes last another year. You get the idea. Do whatever it takes.

One of the biggest mistakes entrepreneurs make is acting out of pride and giving up too soon. I have seen a number of viable businesses fail in this manner. There will be pain. There will be disappointments and you will fall flat on your face more times than you would like to admit. You will take two steps back before you can take three steps forward.

Unless you are absolutely certain without a sliver of a doubt that God has positively slammed the door in your face, stick it out. Make it work. It is, after all, up to you. It is your <u>vision</u> that will keep you going. In my industry, there is nothing intrinsically exciting about mopping a floor at midnight. Think, however, of a vision of building a large cleaning service creating mutually beneficial relationships with customers, employees and vendors. Consider multiplying this vision through franchises that enable honest and hard-working men and women a means to honor and glorify God through their work. Now THAT is exciting.

I can do everything through

him who gives me strength.

Philippians 4:13 (NIV)

Chapter Eight
Tame Your Anxiety

Have you ever gone for a ride on a roller coaster? If you are like me, the instant the car tugs forward your inner voice begins to whine. What made you get on this infernal contraption just to get hurled and tossed around? You make a gallant attempt to look cool and in control. As the car climbs up the incline, higher and higher, your hysterical inner voice keeps rattling off, your heart beats faster, and your fingers wrap tightly around the safety bar. At this time, you begin to prepare for what's ahead. You might do well to remember to hold on to your baseball hat and tuck your sunglasses in your pocket. You mentally brace yourself for the fall. For it inevitably comes. Now it happens, a hair-raising free fall. Every doubt you had about getting on the ride is confirmed. Strangely, after the second or third drop, you begin to conquer your anxiety. Your inner voice goes silent. Time is moving slower. You belong with the flow of the moment. You are having fun! The highs and lows are now expected and enjoyable. And then, you are sad to see the ride come to an end. In fact, you even consider jumping right back in line to start over again.

Being an entrepreneur is not unlike riding a roller coaster. You'd better hold on real tight. Most people experience highs and lows in their jobs. For an entrepreneur, the highs are exquisitely higher and the lows are crushingly lower. When you are in the thick of it, you will question your very decision of going into business by yourself. This is the time to hold on to your hat and brace yourself mentally for the fall.

Once you tame the anxiety and you incorporate the lows as part of the bigger process of operating a business, you will keep seeking more and more of the roller coaster. We all crave excitement, and owning our own business is a very good place to find it. The extreme entrepreneur will even "shake things up a little" if the going gets too smooth. Give your body and mind time to adjust to the rigors of your trade. Not only will your excitement show, it will also entice others to become part of the ride with you.

Now let me share a secret with you. The time will come when you will realize that even the lowest point in your career as an entrepreneur will take you to a higher place by comparison than any of the highest points you could ever experience in a job working for somebody else. I call it the point where the "paying the dues" stage is over. As an employee there is a ceiling to your achievements, dictated by your job description and by the caliber of the management above you. As an entrepreneur you are vibrating at a higher wavelength. Your ceiling is wide open. Your only limit is your ability to expand your own vision. This is the future that you can look forward to.

Chapter Nine
Never get Too Impressed with Yourself

As much as you dread the lows in your business life, you are absolutely thrilled with its peaks. You love the rush of securing that important contract, maybe getting the "Business of the Year Award" or simply basking in the recognition you receive in your community as a symbol of success. If you ever get to the point where you are really satisfied and impressed with yourself, be careful! "Pride goes before destruction, and a haughty spirit before a fall" (Proverbs, 16:18).

But isn't this the whole point? Isn't all your hard work aiming to that moment when you look behind and ahead of you and what you see makes you feel really proud of how far you've come? There is nothing wrong with taking pride in one's work. In fact, business places no premiums on timidity. Self-assurance and confidence in your knowledge and abilities will help you make headway. Just make sure you give the credit to God. Your great business success would be meaningless without Him. It is God who has blessed you with the ability to work, to think, to listen, to physically walk through a door and meet with a customer. Give God the praise and you may very well discover that He is not done yet. We all answer to God one day, so make sure you handle failure and success in their proper measure.

So how do you keep your pride under good regulation? Pat yourself on the back for a job well done, enjoy your successes and make sure to share your joy with others. Say "thank you" to your customers, your vendors, your employees, your bank and most importantly - God. Watch out for arrogance and self-importance. These are the sins to which great and gifted men are most susceptible. Most importantly, don't stop doing what got you to the top. The roller coaster is still there! And we can only coast downhill!

Chapter Ten
Turn Problem into Process

I grew up in Crockett Mills, a small town in the rural cotton country of West Tennessee. Every year my mom and dad planted a big garden behind our house. It covered almost one acre. From an early age, I got to help and learned many valuable lessons in the process. While dad was at work, my mom would tend the garden. She took great pride in her garden and carefully selected the best spot for it – high enough to prevent flooding and with just the right amount of sunshine.

One year, something very strange happened. Weeds began to pop up and grow all over the place. They were choking the life out of our precious vegetables. My Mom could have done one of several things:

a) She could have sat on the couch with her head in her hands and just given up.

b) She could have handed me a $20 dollar bill and rushed me over to the hardware store to buy a hoe.

c) She could have had a hoe in the shed from day one to be used precisely in such cases.

As it turns out, my mom was an option C type. She had the hoe leaning against the shed, at the ready. She took care of the weeds right then and there. Just as we could see her triumph taking shape, a drought hit. Three weeks without rain. Would you believe that my mom threw her arms up in the air and vowed never to plant a garden again? You know a little about my mom by now. She surely did not. She watered the garden twice a day. She had the hose ready, long enough to reach the farthest corners. We enjoyed delicious vegetables all summer.

Consider this: my mom did not look at weeds or droughts as "PROBLEMS." She looked at these occurrences as part of the "PROCESS" of successfully tending a garden. These things happen and there was nothing she could do about it. What she did have control over, however, was her response. She was well informed and well prepared; she took these matters in stride.

Being in a labor intensive industry, the Office Pride approach is the same toward all the events in our business. Take employee turnover for example. We do not consider it a "PROBLEM", but simply part of the "PROCESS" of growing a successful janitorial service.

We are proactive and hire while we are strong and at our best rather than wait until the last minute when we would be short-handed and desperate. The success of this approach was made clear during a visit to a trade show one year. As companies in our industry gathered from throughout the country, a pervasive theme developed: growth had become impossible over the past year because the American work-force had deteriorated to an alarming level.

Many participants dwelled on the abhorrent lack of work ethics of the average employee. They had foregone opportunities to gain new customers because "good employees" were simply not available. Most companies I talked to repeated the same litany of misfortunes. Their sales had either decreased or remained stagnant during the past year.

Within our Office Pride delegation we looked at each other in disbelief. We approached labor issues just as weeds in the garden. We viewed them as part of growing a business and did not allow them to get us down. We had grown 57% that year, an excellent harvest.

Take a page from my mom's gardening book: be well informed and well prepared, eliminate the word "PROBLEM" from your vocabulary and think in terms of "PROCESS" instead.

I really believe it is a choice. As an entrepreneur, you can choose to be either "PROBLEM" focused or "PROCESS" focused. The exhibit in this chapter outlines the differences between the two. Read through the exhibit and get reinforced to choose success over misery.

You are either:

enduring	**P**ain	or you are	**P**lanning
on the	**R**un	or you are	**R**etaining
hiding behind the	**O**h no!	or standing on the	**O**rganization
creating	**B**ad Attitudes	or	**C**onstructively Building
viewed as a	**L**oser	or as an	**E**xample
you represent the	**E**ndlessly Stressed	or the	**S**tress Free
which leaves you	**M**iserable	or	**S**uccessful

It is your Choice!

"Problem" is **Circumstance** focused.
"Process" is **Vision** focused.

Chapter Eleven
Always say, "Business is Great!"

One of the most critical elements to the success of any business, especially a start-up, is described in the following story. The characters in the story are not real; but the message is a part of my everyday life.

Bob is getting a hair cut and the friendly hairstylist starts a casual conversation. "What do you do for a living?" she asks while competently snipping away. "Oh, I run my own business" says Bob. She acts dutifully impressed and asks Bob how the business is going. Bob does not usually engage in conversation with total strangers but since he is having a particularly trying week, he proceeds to explain how two of his key employees got sick at the same time and how he had to cover for them working two nights in a row around the clock to get caught up. She keeps nodding sympathetically while putting in the finishing touches and Bob is very pleased with his reflection in the mirror. She did a good job. As Bob gets up his next-door neighbor comes in to take his place. "How's business, buddy?" he chirps. "Not too bad, I guess..." Bob quips as he waves good-bye.

Now the hair-stylist engages Bob's neighbor in friendly conversation while promptly getting to work. She noticed that he and Bob knew each other so she proceeds to relate the details about the dreadful week that poor Bob just had. In his mind Bob's neighbor simply hears that the business is not doing well and that Bob is overwhelmed and can't take it any more.

"No wonder he didn't sound enthusiastic, poor soul," he comments. "My sister-in-law is one of Bob's best clients, I guess I'd better warn her." Bob is oblivious to the ripple effect that his little conversation had as he goes about his day, looking sharp with his new haircut.

A similar scenario could happen at any time, in any number of ways. Your friends and family know that you started a business, so naturally when they see you the innocent little question comes up: "How's business?" If you respond in a negative or even neutral fashion, your response will snowball and people will lose confidence in you very quickly. In our culture, people feed off the negative. By sharing the bad that is happening in your business, you are "shooting yourself in the foot" and you are sending a horrible message out to your current and prospective customers.

No matter how bad your business is doing, or how rough it gets for you, always say: "Business is great! We have great customers and great employees. We are always looking for more good customers and more good employees!" Say it with a smile in your voice and look straight into their eyes. Next thing you know, the word is spreading about how your business is a success. As potential customers and employees hear this, they want to become part of your success story. You are, in fact, feeding your own growth with your good attitude.

If you are looking for encouragement, just wait until people start coming up to you saying that they heard your business is doing really well. This has happened to me many times, sometimes when I had just had the worst day of my business life. Those words were just what I needed to get through another day. Try it. It is more fun than telling people about all the negative things that are going on. They really don't want to hear your whining anyway; they have concerns of their own. So feed them the good news and let them go to work for you!

Chapter Twelve
Dig Deep to Meet Your Cash-Flow Needs

As I am sitting down to write this chapter, I just got off the phone with my dear friend Lisa. She was barely able to hold back her tears. At the current pace her business is going, Lisa will not be able to make payroll in three weeks. Quite a grim prospect.

Lisa's business had experienced rapid sales success early on. Growth requires cash and her cash was gone. It was time to camp out a little and get caught up on cash-flow. I encouraged Lisa to hang in there. I suggested that she sit down and do a detailed and deep analysis of absolutely all of her resources (this is the part of the roller-coaster ride where you sit tight and hold on to your hat). This is mostly a time for sacrifice, as any successful business owner knows who stuck it out in his own time.

Those unwelcome words, "you must pay your dues," suddenly ring truer than ever, dues-meaning your cash, other assets and lots of sweat equity. I can relate to how Lisa must be feeling. I once worked at an International Fraternity as a traveling consultant. During one particular year, I traveled to fifty-five different colleges, spending three days on each campus working with the local fraternity leaders in areas such as leadership development and community service.

One fond memory I have of that year is the vehicle I was driving. An awesome, powerful, midnight-blue Ford Bronco II 4X4. I loved my truck. This truck and I had traveled the whole country together and it had also been useful when I began the cleaning service. But then the going got tough for my business and it was time to look around at my assets. The list included my wife's old car, my beautiful Bronco and the company van which I had bought used for $5,000.

The decision was painful, but obvious. I took my beloved Bronco to the nearest used car lot and cashed it in for $3,200. I also held a yard sale and sold a number of our household items including our handsome antique mahogany dining room table and eight chairs built during the Great Depression. This gave a whole new meaning to the words "putting food on the table." We managed to bring in enough money to enable my business to stay alive for another two months. It was just the two months we needed for Office Pride to reach "break-even" for the first time.

Before you give in to despair, take inventory of all your resources. You may have more than you know. Don't forget your family. If you are truly working as hard as you can and using your money wisely, don't be afraid to ask capable family members and friends to participate. Help may come forth in the shape of a low or "no-interest" loan.

Or you might decide to trade some equity in your company for an injection of cash. Just be careful not to give up too big of a share of your company. It is probably worth more than you know. Remember, they are not investing in what you are now; but what you are going to create. They are investing in you!

Take a good look around. You can do it.

Chapter Thirteen
Understand the Numbers

The ceaseless demands on our time often tempt us into taking shortcuts. We scan the newspaper and zap through the cable channels. A number of business owners treat their financial statements the same way. They really have no idea whether they are losing or making money on any given day. Usually, they only pay attention when the numbers slide into the red. As much as I hate to admit, I was like this during my first few years in business. Taking care of customers was so important that I often used that responsibility as an admiral excuse to not spend the time needed to understand the critical numbers within my company.

By the very nature of being an entrepreneur, it is natural for me to find sales and operations more interesting than the administrative side of the business. Personally, I would much rather be visiting an account or negotiating with a vendor than entering data to produce profit and loss reports. I would gladly delegate this task to someone else. It took me ten years to realize the importance of gathering and analyzing this information in a timely manner. Moreover, I am now experienced enough to know that the only good financial statements are those I can thoroughly understand, the simpler the better. What good does a sophisticated multi-colored chart do if you cannot grasp where the numbers came from and how they may affect your business?

On the flip side, when times are good we may let our guard down as long as money is in the bank or as long as there have been no collection calls. There is much more to good financial management than figuring out how to make payroll on Friday.

Here is an exercise I recommend to anyone running their own business. Whether you have a board of advisors or just a group of trusted friends or associates to take their place. Have them review your financial statements and ask you questions. You should be able to find your answers quickly and accurately. The simple exercise of preparing for this meeting will give you a self-learning opportunity and make your company much stronger for it.

Most money is made and lost behind the scenes. Well-managed money can make you money. You need to make informed decisions quickly and be able to react to unexpected events with confidence. In my organization, the bookkeeping is delegated, but I have total control over what the numbers mean. In this way, I can spot an irregularity before it turns into a devastating financial loss.

Set aside time each week to just review your finances and critical numbers. It is a must if you are serious about long-term survival.

Chapter Fourteen
Have a Plan B

You have heard the advice to "burn your ships" if you want to be successful. This school of thought urges you to launch forward making sure there is no way for you to turn back. It further dissuades you from devising a Plan B - the reason being that if you don't have an alternate route you would be forced to make Plan A work at all costs. This is disastrous advice!

I not only always have a Plan B but many times I also keep a Plan C and D at hand; to be whipped out in case of need. If Plan A is not effective, I am already prepared with a constructive alternative. Not only that, but you may find that it is Plan C that gets you where you wanted to go in the first place. An added advantage of following this practice is that once you follow the discipline to develop several plans right from the start you will end up with a well thought out and more comprehensive Plan A.

Are you ready to hear another bonus? Beyond the benefit of strategic planning, having a Plan B also gives you the inner strength to be an effective leader in your daily operational areas. Let's say you are having trouble with Hank, an employee who generally falls short of quality expectations and, adding worse to bad enough, consistently shows up late for work. Once he gets to work, Hank acts defensively and tries to avoid you. The catch is that Hank is in charge of collections on overdue accounts and you frankly hate doing this yourself. The mere thought of picking up the phone to call a client to remind them that they owe you money simply makes your insides churn.

Therefore, you have never confronted Hank as you should have, simply because you dread having to fill in for him if he quits.

Here is a perfect occasion for Plan B. You start cross-training another employee in your accounting department who is diligent and seems eager to learn. You show him every aspect of Hank's responsibilities. Soon, this employee is ready to fill Hank's shoes, if so required. Knowing you have this alternative gives you the courage and peace of mind to confront Hank. Once you do, you feel a weight lifting off your shoulders. You have no control over Hank's reaction, but you do have a response ready whether he decides to fall in line and correct his actions or leave. Your employees will respect your leadership and everyone will be glad that the problem employee is no longer a disrupting factor.

So rather than "burn your ships", I say keep a back-up armada on the docks - ready to launch on short notice.

Chapter Fifteen
Be "Strategically Correct"

Many young businesses have never experienced the effects of a recession. As part of the natural cycle of any economy, recessions happen in
varying degrees of severity. I had always basked in
the general belief that the janitorial industry is
recession-proof. An economic slowdown could
only mean more good workers looking for part-
time employment, which is good news for us.
However, I was enlightened by an industry veter-
an who plainly asked me one day, "Have you con-

sidered the impact of a recession on Office Pride?" His question came out of nowhere, and after I mumbled something about being recession-proof I quickly realized, by his raised eyebrows, that my reply was not making an impression on this man. I felt that God was sending me a message through him.

He gruffly fired the next question, "Well, can you afford to lose half your customers?" The answer was clearly "no, we could not". Not only could we not afford to lose half of our royalty base, but our franchise owners could not afford to lose half of their customer base either. This wise man shared his experience with me. During the recession of 1983, he had lost half his business because he had not been prepared. So much for my recession-proof industry! His customers had cancelled or cut back services in an effort to survive themselves.

I took due note and immediately worked on a plan to prepare ourselves and our franchise owners for such a situation. The better prepared we are and the better we prepare our internal customers and vendors, the less a recession will hurt us. For this purpose I involved advisors who had experienced a recession in our industry, and identified actions that we could take today, in order to strengthen our position tomorrow. I presented the plan to the staff in such a way that they would view it as a strategically smart exercise, as opposed to a vision of impending doom. The shape of such an action strategy greatly depends on the industry. Our plan involved many aspects of our operation. Here are a few examples:

- Be proactive about knowing our customers and how their businesses are doing. Perform quarterly customer reviews.

- If a customer shows signs of trouble or decrease in size, be there for them, and offer them temporary consultative cost cutting solutions.

- Aim at 100% customer retention. Earn their trust and reinforce it continuously. Act on customer loss immediately to regain the account or replace the business.

- Implement a proprietary program to benchmark industry-wide customer satisfaction. Provide competitive comparison information both to potential customers to obtain new business, as well as to existing customers to prompt them to generate referrals.

- Involve employees in the identification of cost-reduction measures.
- Maximize utilization of current staff and office resources.
- Qualify sales leads to increase effectiveness of sales time.
- Keep cash available and monitor cash position daily. Do not max out the line of credit.
- Provide key indicators to each staff member to monitor individual performance. We call these "critical numbers"!
- Measure profit on a weekly basis, not monthly. (Depending on the nature and size of your business, daily measures may be more appropriate.)

I am grateful that I had this early warning to give me time to prepare and therefore minimize the impact of a recession on our organization. In generating your own plan make sure you involve the stakeholders upstream and downstream from your business. Also make sure that you don't create a bottleneck by underestimating growth, in case the recession takes longer than expected to arrive. Should the economic slowdown not come when expected, a solid strategic plan will not only make you stronger, but will enable you to benefit even more, for as long as the good times last.

Having this plan in place positioned Office Pride to grow 80% during the economic slump or recession in 2001 and 2002.

Chapter Sixteen
Test your Back Up

It may now sound like an April Fool's story, but it really happened to me. Most businesses keep a digital back-up copy of their financial data, and so did mine. On one infamous day, our entire financial computer base crashed. It only took one mistake by a user with access to cause the debacle. We had seven back-up tapes, one for each day of the week. It seemed that we were in pretty good shape, we would only lose one or two hours worth of work. Or so I thought.

Our network consultant proceeded to inform me that for the last year we had, for reasons unknown to human logic, backed-up a shortcut file instead of the complete thing. I could feel my blood turning cold as I was further exposed to the facts - these tapes had never been tested in an off-site computer and they now appeared to be blank. As the realization sank in that we would never recover the information, we jumped to our feet and got to work feverishly around the clock. At Office Pride, when we get knocked down, we dust ourselves off and keep going. This attitude has seen us through more than one crisis. In this case, we did contain the damage, and very few people ever found out. It took enormous effort, and the cost in time and money was considerable - I call it our $100,000 computer lesson. As you can imagine, my entire attitude towards our back-up procedures changed that day. I still delegate the task to a computer network consultant; but today I make sure that the system is tested, and I am not satisfied until I see it with my own eyes.

Often when I ask other CEO's about their

computer back-up they either sit on the edge of their chair and admit that they have never had it tested or they confidently assure me that it is under control, then discretely jot a note to themselves in their calendar. When it comes to your most valuable data, you cannot afford to assume. It is my hope that sharing my expensive lesson will spare you from going through the same kind of agony.

Chapter Seventeen
Pay Attention to Red Flags when Hiring

You know it. I know you do. I knew it too. Not everyone will tell you the truth. Do you recognize any of the following?

1) "The check is in the mail".
2) "Your call is important to us, please hold".
3) "I'm from the government and I'm here to help you".

Similarly, many (if not most) job applicants will lie about one thing or another at some point in the hiring process. The simple task of checking references will prove that most applications contain some degree of falsehood. I always knew this, but I still had to learn my lesson the hard way. I hired people that I suspected of not telling the full truth, because I thought I could help them. This was a big mistake.

I have a rule of thumb to never hire a candidate who arrives late for an interview (red flag). On one occasion a young man from Indiana arrived for an interview twenty minutes late. He explained that he had trouble finding the building. I had a flash-back to my job-hunting days as a student. Whenever I interviewed for jobs away from campus, I would find the location one hour early and give myself plenty of time to arrive at the agreed upon place a few minutes ahead of schedule. Against my best instincts, however, I decided to give this young man a chance because I knew his dad; saying to myself that in every other respect he was an acceptable candidate. I hired him and assigned him to an important account.

The disappointment didn't take long to come. He soon left the company and shortly thereafter we came across a most disturbing find. He had stolen a credit card number from the unsuspecting CEO's secretary, and had used it to make a considerable number of expensive "phone-sex" calls. That day I promised myself to listen more carefully to my instincts. Valuable employees who have a good track record and are proud of their performance will show up to an interview on time.

Now, when candidates show up late for an interview, I inform them of my policy and ask them if they would still like to talk. Most hastily walk away probably feeling violated in their right to waste my time. In amused retrospect, I reflect that if they found it so easy to arrive late to a meeting with their future boss, they would just as easily arrive late to a meeting with our customer.

Another rule of thumb is to hire people based on their past and not on what they claim their future is likely to be. This is one case where you can say that past performance is your best predictor of future behavior. Moreover, you haven't got much else on which to base your assessment.

I once had a young man from Kentucky come in for an interview. As is customary, I asked him for his references. He seemed concerned about the fact that since all his references were from out of state, I would be incurring long distance charges to call them. Once he completed his application, I noted that he had listed his address as a motel in Greenwood, Indiana. He accounted for this fact with a convincing story. He also laid out his well-prepared plans for the future and how the job we had available would fit right in. It only took one reference check for the deception to come undone. The young man was on the run with a 15-year-old girl. The county sheriff and his entire hometown in Kentucky were looking for him.

Along the same lines, beware of the candidate whose references don't call you back. People who have good things to say will gladly call you back. If they don't, then there probably is something they would rather not talk about. Take the hint. My goal is to get four good references. Getting no response definitely does not count.

I cannot stress enough the importance of

choosing your employees well. It is, after all, these individuals who will represent you and your company. They will be the face of your business before clients and vendors. They will become the defining image of your brand in the market. Your responsibility is to build and safeguard your brand in every possible way. Hiring the right people is a truly excellent way to start.

When encouragement is what you need, surround yourself with men and women whose quality of work will encourage you and not leave you drained. At Office Pride, God has blessed us with truly great and wonderful people, both qualified and committed. This has given me great peace and joy. It took a lot of persistence, time, mistakes and hard work to build our team. It has been worth it!

Chapter Eighteen
Pay Attention and Bless Your People Behind the Scenes

A great way to be encouraged as a business owner is to seize opportunities to bless others. The following story highlights one business owner who took advantage of a golden opportunity.

The Holiday Season is here. Shopping is in the air. Everybody is excited and busy planning, decorating and celebrating. Except for Larry. He is having the worst Christmas of his life. Larry is one of the best employees in his company. He is reliable, competent and just plain fun to be with. His cheerful attitude always gives a lift to those around him. But today he is really quiet. Larry has just suffered a pretty serious setback.

Last payday he went out to run a couple of errands and tucked $350, the rent money, carefully in his wallet. The rest of the pay would buy Christmas gifts for his little girl. She had penned an eager letter to Santa which he kept in his wallet too. It made him chuckle every time he thought of her tiny hand-writing. This year he would be able to get her pretty much everything on her list. Except when Larry got home, the carefully folded money was gone. He had no idea of when or where he could have dropped it. He backtracked through each and every one of his steps that day. Nothing. Suddenly, there was not enough money for both rent and Christmas gifts. His little girl wouldn't understand, and his wife was sure to be upset.

Larry's boss always paid attention to her employees and noticed something was not quite right. She casually asked around and learned of Larry's plight. She knew Larry to be a careful and trustworthy man. He would hardly make a careless mistake like this. When the end of year bonus was distributed the following day, Larry was awestruck to find that his envelope contained much more than he could ever expect. In fact, it contained $350 - exactly the amount of money he had lost! His eyes welled with tears as he went up to his boss to privately thank her. No one else knew of her gesture. She had blessed him quietly and behind the scenes. Larry remained a trusted employee, more loyal now than ever before.

Larry's name is not real but his story is. Larry and his boss both believe that the missing money probably went to someone who was having a lot of trouble and had been praying really hard to God for help and had suddenly found a wad of cash just lying there! It was an answered prayer. How many times have you heard stories like this from the receiving end. Someone needed money, prayed and the next day there it was in the mailbox. In this case, Larry and his boss were on the giving side. Larry's story reminded me that God is at work and sometimes he may choose our business as an instrument in His infinite wisdom. Be sensitive to these types of opportunities. As your participation blesses and encourages others, you will be blessed and encouraged in return.

Chapter Nineteen
Always Take the High Road

Any able business leader needs to recognize deception and protect his organization from it. Vendors who may misrepresent their product, customers who do not intend to pay, employees who hide their backgrounds, they all pose a danger to business survival.

The most treacherous kind of deception is the one we inflict upon ourselves. How much would you say your integrity is worth? Would you give it up for $300? Or maybe $300,000? If you had asked this question to Henry (not his real name), a good man I once knew, he never would have believed his integrity was worth only $2,700. And yet, it came to that. Are you wondering how I know the exact dollar figure? I just asked him one question. Let me share the story with you.

Henry was the owner of a service business that was doing rather well. He was a honest, hard-working man. One day one of his customers called to inform him that $3,000 worth of tools were missing from his office. He suspected that one of Henry's employees had taken them. The suspicion was confirmed when the particular employee did not show up for work the next day, and any further doubt dissipated when Henry found that the suspect had a theft record. Henry had not done his due diligence before hiring this employee, as he knew he should have. The customer did not press charges, but expected Henry to take responsibility and replace the stolen tools.

Henry was very troubled and came to me for advice. He first related the facts and then followed with his own interpretation. Since the police had not pursued the case it may mean that someone else might have taken the tools, and in any case, since they were used they may not be worth $3,000. And Henry did not have that kind of money available anyway, so how could the customer expect him to replace the tools? His reasoning had become so muddled that he even started blaming the customer for leaving the tools lying about in plain view.

Henry had evidently not come to me for advice but for validation of the decision he had already made. I only asked him one question. "Henry, if the tools had been worth $300, would you replace them?" "Of course I would"!, he said, because he could afford the $300. My advice to Henry was that the $2,700 difference had no impact on right from wrong. In his heart he knew what was the right thing to do.

Sadly, Henry betrayed his integrity and chose not to compensate the customer. I saw him again about five months later. Riddled with guilt and anger, he had let his business deteriorate until it finally closed.

Always take the high road. You are only given your integrity once. If you give it up for sale, neither fortune nor fame will ever be able to buy it back for you again.

You are the salt of the earth. But if the salt loses its saltiness, how can it be made salty again? It is no longer good for anything, except to be thrown out and trampled by men.

Matthew 4:13 (NIV)

Chapter Twenty
Be a Friend to Your Vendor

God's word says that believers are to be the salt of the earth. Trying to live up to His mandate has enriched many areas of my business life, in particular, my relationship with vendors. If we are to build and maintain the strength required to raise and keep our product at the highest levels, we must cooperate with our vendors and be to them the kind of customer that we aspire to have.

This requires finding vendors who share an understanding of the cardinal principles that rule your business. It is not uncommon, while you are still a newcomer to the industry, for your vendors to know more about your business than you do. Getting along with them and building a strong relationship will give you plenty of opportunities to get ahead. Here is one simple thing I do to please my vendors: I pay my bills early! So my bookkeeper says I can wait until the 30th of the month? I send in my payment as soon as I can. The same goes for the rest of my suppliers. My vendors get three distinct messages:

1) I am reliable.
2) I care about them.
3) My business is doing well.

Now, think of the message that we send when we do not pay our bills on time.

Beyond fulfilling the sacred mandate to be "salt of the earth", there are various secular advantages to paying your bills early. Whenever I have a last minute request, and I admit it happens more often than I would wish, my vendors invariably respond because they know I would do the same for them and they also know they will get paid right away.

Many times the opportunity to get a new customer rests on my ability to obtain a quick response on a special request. If I didn't have the support from my vendors in these cases, or if I couldn't rely on their willingness to go the extra mile for me, these opportunities would most likely pass me by.

At Office Pride, we have always considered our vendors to be as critically important to our success as our customers. Each of us is a stakeholder in the grander scheme of our overall prosperity. A good way to measure our success is by the benefits others have gained from it. Without customers, we would not have a business - without vendors, we could not serve our customers. As the proverb goes: "one hand cannot applaud alone".

Chapter Twenty-one
Do not make Excuses

You know how things go, when what we are working on starts to fall apart? We send out the signal, loud and clear, that it isn't our fault! We justify our shortcomings by pointing the accusing finger in some other direction. There is an infinite number of excuses we can summon, whether real or imaginary, to satisfy the need to place responsibility elsewhere.

This reminds me of Mike (name substitution), one of our franchise owners. The labor situation had been very good for most of our franchisees, with turnover below average, which usually leads to less headaches and more profit. Mike, however, called me to complain that he would not be able to start two new jobs because he couldn't find and keep quality help. He had many different "reasons" why this was happening; one good employee had left to work for the competition, he had lost a good candidate because of insurance and so the list went on. I suspected that the issue, in this case, was the owner, so I told him to do a self-analysis of his hiring and training practices. It seemed painfully obvious to me that he had either stopped checking references, or had taken shortcuts in the training program, both leading to increased turnover. While Mike whined, I concentrated on how to fix the problem, rather than who was to blame for it. We had made a commitment to the new customers and we needed to keep it. Another franchise owner was ready and pitched in to take over the two jobs for us. He had proactively trained some friends to help in such a situation. His foresight gave him a chance to turn crisis into opportunity and to grow his business as a result.

Just as I discussed in Chapter 10, once you identify what your "problems" are and you view them as part of the "process", you must proactively put in place a procedure to minimize or eliminate the occurrence. The solution usually starts with looking at how to change yourself. An older preacher, so the story goes, was once asked by a younger preacher how he could keep his congregation wide awake and attentive during his sermons. The wise preacher replied that he always had a man watch for sleepers, with instructions, as soon as he saw anyone start nodding or dozing, to hasten to the pulpit and wake up the preacher! Aren't we usually less sensible? Wouldn't we be inclined to have the watcher wake up, not ourselves, but the people he caught sleeping? Most of us are uncomfortable about confronting our own weak areas.

I have heard a number of business owners boast of how they get rid of problem customers. By this they mean, of course, that they got rid of those customers who had dared complain. With few exceptions, customers generally complain for legitimate reasons. For my part, I appreciate a customer who will call to express dissatisfaction more than one who will not communicate with me, and just cancel the service without warning. At least the former gave me a chance to correct the situation and improve my operation. I am the steward of my business; if not me, who will make the decisions required to lead, motivate and grow my team of people?

The French are fond of the expression: *"Qui s'excuse s'accuse"* (He who excuses himself, accuses himself). Next time you point your finger at someone else, notice that there are three fingers in your hand still pointing back at you.

Why do you look at the speck of sawdust in your brother's eye and pay no attention to the plank in your own eye?

Matthew 7:3 (NIV)

Chapter Twenty-two
Finish Each Day

You already have your one-year strategy and you most likely have a three-year or five-year plan as well. What is sometimes overlooked is that a year is made of days and the days are made of hours. The way that you spend each of these hours is what ultimately leads you to reach your target. Apply strategic thinking to your day. Start the morning with a list of tasks you want to accomplish in their order of importance (this is a list you prepared the night before).

Tackle the items at the top of your list first, and the hours will naturally yield accomplishments. Otherwise, you are likely to get sidetracked by events and end up spending your time aimlessly. Occasionally, when your day starts on the rough side, you will experience what I call a "mental gear shift"; from productive to depressed. The hours start slipping away into a void, while you stare blankly at the wall. When you start thinking this way, you need to recognize that your brain will appease and sooth your "mental gear shift" until you persuade yourself that this is how the day was supposed to go anyway. You may find yourself stopping for a cup of coffee or just driving around until it's time to go back home. Suddenly the guilt may lift as you justify your spontaneous round of golf as "networking" or you use the excuse that a little rain makes a perfect day to not go out "cold calling" after all.

I have experienced this at times. I have started the day with five items on the list and when task number one proves to be too difficult, I jump on to complete the other four. That is the equivalent of going grocery shopping for Thanksgiving and bringing home everything but the turkey! If you are to get only one task done from your list, make sure it is the top one. The same principle applies to your monthly, quarterly and yearly goals. Once you learn to finish your day, the natural progression will lead you into a productive path of attainment of your long-term goals.

Chapter Twenty-three
Invest in Yourself

Just as a fine engine needs continuous tuning, so do you and your leadership skills. As your company grows, you need to remain one step ahead. Either you keep up, or else the forces of entropy will catch up with you, sooner than you think.

I often hear my fellow entrepreneurs state that they don't need to waste their time attending a seminar or conference because they have "heard it all before." Perhaps their perception of their own perfection cannot endure the insult. Do you know what I tell them? Unless everything, and I mean everything, runs flawlessly (and it hardly ever does) they need to hear it all again.

For myself, I am an eager participant, always open to learn, so I take every opportunity to attend these leadership development events. Granted, it is not easy to set aside the time and put a busy schedule on hold. But I find that I would hardly have the authority to ask my managers and employees to expand their ability and skills unless I am willing to set these same goals for myself.

Here is another way I keep learning: I hire people that are better at what they do than I am. When I hire a sales manager, I hire one who is better at closing deals than I am. For a bookkeeper, I look for someone who is more organized than I am. The Customer Service Manager needs to be more patient and caring than I am. In this way, I keep growing and pushing myself to new heights to live up to my end of the deal: to set the course for them to follow, and to inspire and motivate them along the way.

As a leader, once you have set the course and you have assembled a group of qualified and self-actualizing people, you will be able to get where you want to go. You may need to adjust the course at times. After all, if you don't find a way to do your job better, somebody else will. Keep an open mind to learn from others and invest in tuning your own engine so that you can enjoy long-lived success and a prosperous business.

Chapter Twenty-four
Train Through the Trials

I have coached Little League baseball for many years. Several years ago one of my little "trainees", Ben, was having a really hard time learning to catch and the rest of the team was leaving him behind. There was not much I could do, except encourage him and give him some basic pointers.

Every time the ball headed in Ben's direction the whole team cringed. Ben's teammates, as kid's often do, let him know in no uncertain terms that he needed to improve. Ben couldn't have tried any harder. I felt like running up and hugging him every time he walked off the field in tears. And then one day before a big game, Ben came up to me and confessed that he was thinking of quitting, although he loved to play. He just couldn't take the teasing from his friends any more. I tried to offer some reassurance and told Ben to take a little time to think it over, trying not to pressure him into a decision.

I was surprised to see Ben show up the next week, and then the next. Something inside him had changed. This little boy was growing up in front of my eyes. A few weeks later he started to improve. Although not destined to become a star on the team, he eventually caught up with the rest and had enormous fun playing from then on. Many summers later, a deep voice from across the street called out, "Coach!" It was Ben, now a six-foot tall handsome young man. He asked me if I remembered his struggle in Little League. "You know?" he said, "I learned a lesson back then, it was so tough to face the other kids, but I just decided not to quit and it turned out Okay, don't you think?" Ben told me that his lesson in perseverance came in handy in high school. He was not the fastest learner, but he worked hard and made good grades. Ben showed me a letter from the University of Memphis. He had just been accepted with a full scholarship. He was brimming with promise.

As a firm believer in formal schooling, I used to roll my eyes at the common belief that the best education comes from the school of hard knocks. But I have to admit that some life skills can hardly be learned any other way. How else could Ben learn about perseverance, but from overcoming repeated defeat? I have certainly learned a few tough lessons, some I have shared with you, like the computer crash or hiring the wrong people.

God gives us this wisdom in Hebrews 12:11 "No discipline seems pleasant at the time, but painful. Later on, however, it produces a harvest of righteousness and peace for those who have trained in it." Notice the catch - we only benefit from the pain if we allow ourselves to be trained by it. It is often hard to see this while we are in the middle of the lesson - all we want is for the pain to stop. Next time you are in a difficult situation, I encourage you to consider it a lesson in self-control and learn what you can from the experience. Learn, learn, and never stop learning. Count your entrepreneurial trials as investments in yourself that will later produce a copious return, molding you into a high-caliber leader.

Chapter Twenty-five
Compost Your Failures to Fertilize Success

The young man asked the successful business-man, "What is the key to your success? "Good decisions" was the wise old man's reply. "And how did you learn to make good decisions?" the young man prodded. "Experience" said the old man. "Where did you get the experience?" the young man asked eagerly. "Bad decisions!" replied the old man.

Eldon Kibbey, a friend of mine, is a dedicated gardener. As we sat in his backyard one evening, I marveled at his beautiful lawn. "Eldon, you can truthfully say that the grass is greener on your side of the fence!" At this, we both pondered on how many people think about changing jobs, careers, businesses, or even wives, believing that the grass will be greener on the other side. Eldon referred me to Psalm 37:3 "Trust in the Lord and do good: dwell in the land and enjoy safe pasture." Eldon reasons that what we need to do is stay on our side and make the grass greener wherever we are.

Eldon uses his leaves, spent flowers, and other garden refuse for compost, to be incorporated into the sticky Indiana soil and to gradually improve it. The compost is dead, but it contains the nutrients that will support future growth. He drew a parallel with business.

Tough experiences can provide the "nutrients" for future success. He was reminded of his experience during a bee-keeping project in high-school. He started with one bee-hive, then two, and then the County Agent asked him if he wanted to buy out a local beekeeper, so he ended up with 10 hives. Eldon learned a lot about "mergers and acquisitions" from that experience. He found that the hives and equipment were dirty and poorly maintained. He spent a lot of time painting and repairing the hive bodies and cleaning the frames. He consolidated some weaker hives, to make stronger, more productive units.

One day, when he walked up to a hive to clean up the equipment, he found a tangled mess of honeycomb in a box. The bees were frustrated and angry! Eldon got stung 15 times before he could get out, and had a similar experience when he returned with the proper equipment. Unfortunately, he had to kill the bees, but managed to salvage the honey in the hive. Eldon said he learned early-on that buying someone else's business is a good way to get stung! This lesson saved him a lot of headaches in his business career. He remained leery of buying someone else's "beehives", knowing that there is always a reason why someone is selling a business. There is always an unknown factor, even when there is "full disclosure."

I can't help but appreciate Eldon for going back to the hive and correcting the situation (rather than giving up). He obviously viewed getting stung as part of the process of growing a honey business. When I asked him for another lesson learned from the school of hard knocks, he replied this way, "My attorney once asked me if I knew the difference between education and experience; he said that reading the small print of the contract is education. Not reading it - that's experience." Eldon stopped there, rubbed his head and looked at me, "Do you get the point?" I smiled, then we both turned and continued to admire his green grass.

Chapter Twenty-six
Frequent the Winners Around You

We all need encouragement. Even the suave billionaire, who seemingly walks on water, needs a support structure. Behind a worthy achievement you are likely to find someone who has been encouraged, and behind every encourager you are likely to find some worthy achievement. Encouragement is a spiritual "vitamin" that keeps us going when our energies start to lag. It is worth noting that the amount and quality of encouragement you receive stems from the decisions you make, and the people you choose to frequent.

As an entrepreneur, I urge you to hang out with winners. Winners come in every shape and form; nourishing educators, skillful workers, generous mentors, dedicated athletes, learned intellectuals. People who are inherently satisfied with their lot in life make a valuable contribution to society, which brings them contentment and joy in return. These people shine like beacons. They are winners!

Take my case, for example - I joined the Franklin Chamber of Commerce and found a beacon in Teresa McClure, the Executive Director. Teresa was a source of constant encouragement and sincere praise. She constantly found a positive word to say about my efforts to build Office Pride. Teresa always seemed as excited about Office Pride as I was. Soon I found myself stopping by the Chamber just to say hello, or to drop off some of my brochures. I found nourishment in my brief conversations with Teresa. She hardly suspected that on many of those occasions I was feeling severely discouraged (she wouldn't know of course, because I would always say "Business is Great!"). So many times her words gave me just the lift I needed to see the day through. Teresa is a winner. She had a job to do, and she did it well. Her eyes were open to see the good in others, and underscore it at every opportunity. I am very grateful for her support.

On the opposite side of the spectrum you have the whiners, people who find fault with everything and everyone. Don't underestimate the effect that their gloomy outlook can have on you. Stay away as much as you can. Chances are, if you find yourself hanging out with whiners, you are likely to become one too.

In the long run, whiners never find success. Winners live it!

My dear brothers, take note of this: Everyone should be quick to listen, slow to speak and slow to become angry, for man's anger does not bring about the righteous life that God desires.

James 1:19-20 (NIV)

Chapter Twenty-seven
Refuse to Get Angry

Even harmless things like waiting in line, an overdraft fee at the bank, hunting for a parking spot or a slow line at the supermarket check-out, can make our hearts race. Add to this the additional pressures an entrepreneur normally deals with; problem employees, unpaid debts and customer complaints. There is no getting away from these daily triggers of anger and frustration. As soon as the "red mist" descends, we lose our perspective and say (and do) things that we may later regret. As a result, we may lose a customer, an employee, or even get entangled in a lawsuit.

A study was conducted in Britain recently that yielded some eye-opening results. Eighty-five percent of people interviewed admitted that losing their temper had cost them money. In total the study reports Britons lost £16 billion to temper tantrums. Interestingly enough, the cost split almost evenly for men and women. The most usual targets quoted were dishes, glasses and cars but on many occasions they involved hitting another person. Without going to this extreme, even the mildest display of anger has a cost. It disrupts relationships, hurts and offends sensibilities, and poisons the one who is angered just as much as the victim. If left ungoverned, your flaring temper ends up governing you.

Despite the daily occurrence of rage, very few of us can claim to be dealing with it effectively. Reading the Bible helped me understand that we have a choice in the matter. When anger gets the best of us, we are cracking open the opportunity for Satan to get his foot in the door (Ephesians

4:27). Satan moves quickly and deceives us into doing something we normally would not do. To him, every time we give in to our temper is equivalent to a salesman getting a referral. This is all he needs. Just the introduction is sufficient; a good salesman can take it from there, and before you know it he is closing the deal.

As the master of deception he is, Satan creeps into our lives in this way. Never underestimate his guile. The choice is ours, we have the power to decide that no matter how irritating the circumstances, we will not get angry or frustrated. We can count to ten, or walk out of the room for a minute, and stay calm and logical. Satan is powerless to reach us while we are living in the Peace and Joy of Christ.

Submit yourselves, then, to

God. Resist the devil, and

he will flee from you.

James 4:7

Chapter Twenty-eight
Run Your Own "Encouragement Filter"

Any business day will bring along a string of decisions that need to be made. The nature of those decisions will either leave you feeling encouraged or discouraged. I have a personal system to make as many encouraging decisions as possible. I call it the "Encouragement Filter." When I am faced with a choice, I run it through my encouragement filter to try to imagine how I would feel following the two or more alternative scenarios I am faced with. Once I do this, it is often clear to me which would be the course of action that would make me feel the most encouraged. In other words, it helps me identify the "winning" decision. Let me give you an example:

Just as Austin is finishing the inspection of a cleaning job, he opens a door to a whole area of the office he had not seen before. In dismay he counts three medium-size rooms in considerable disarray. Austin, bone-tired and ready to go home, considers his choices:

a) Clean the overlooked area, even though the customer had failed to include it in the walk-through and was therefore not part of the proposal. He could confirm with the customer the following day if this area should continue to be cleaned in the future.

b) Lock up and go home. The area was not listed in his job sheet, so therefore the job has been completed as noted. He can ask the customer tomorrow if he would like this area to be included in the future. What difference could a day make anyway? The rooms had not been cleaned in some time, to judge by their condition.

Now let's follow these two hypothetical scenarios on to the next morning:

a) Austin calls Ray, the customer. Ray is happy with the work. Austin mentions the additional three rooms and asks if he should keep cleaning them in the future. Ray realizes he had forgotten this area and is relieved that Austin took care of them because, in fact, it is the sales office area, and they are expecting some new customers to come in today. He apologizes to Austin for the oversight and asks him to adjust the invoice to reflect the extra work. He commends Austin on his initiative. All is well.

b) Austin is still in bed. The phone rings - it is Ray, and he is not happy. It so happens that the previous cleaning service was not doing a good job, but the people in the sales office were friendly with the provider, and were against changing. Ray took a stand for Office Pride and assured everyone that it would be a good thing. But when Ray arrived in the office this morning he found the sales people wiping desks and emptying paper bins. They were expecting an important new customer and gleefully exaggerated the failure of the new cleaning service. Austin tried to explain that the sales area was not included in the description. Ray agreed that he forgot to mention it, but explains that the whole situation made him very uncomfortable, too many people were aware of the glitch, and all eyes were on him. Ray said he regretted to do so, but that in order to save face he would have to terminate the agreement with Office Pride and go back to his old cleaning service.

So in this case, the "Encouragement Filter" is easy. If you were in Austin's shoes, you'd much rather go with Scenario A (a happy customer would certainly leave you feeling more encouraged). It is true that many times the choices are not so clear-cut. Even in those cases, the encouragement filter will help you avoid lapses in judgement and identify the "winning decision."

Chapter Twenty-nine
Find Your Peers

It would be hard to pick my best business decision, but if I were to rank my decisions in order of their impact on my success, joining a peer group would certainly be in the top five.

As the struggle of the start-up phase of my business began to ease its grip, I started to face new challenges. On the one hand, as the business took a life of its own, I started to get complacent. At the same time, I was experiencing the proverbial "loneliness" at the top. I had heard of the

Young Entrepreneurs Organization (YEO) and decided to join. In order to qualify as a member you need to be a CEO under 40 years of age, own the majority of your business and have sales of at least $1 Million per year. YEO matched me up with nine other CEO's from non-competing industries. I was amazed at the effect this group had on me. These were bright, young entrepreneurs who were on a journey very similar to mine.

I was no longer alone! Not only would these people become my friends, they would challenge me to grow and think from an entirely different perspective. They thought big, and each of them was growing a business and raising a family, just like me. We were all about the same age and were facing similar circumstances. My peer group supported me when I was down, and provided "big-head therapy" whenever I got too smug and overly confident.

There are many peer groups you can join, such as YEO, Truth @ Work, or the Christian Business Forums of CBMC (Connecting Business Men to Christ), as well as many other industry-specific organizations. Most successful CEO's, even from large corporations, belong to a peer group. These forums provide a safe environment to relate to other business leaders who share the same responsibilities.

You can even create your own peer group. Let's say you own a business in a metropolitan area and you know that you have no plans to expand nationally. You could find similar business owners in other cities where you don't compete with each other. Both time and money can be saved exchanging and pooling resources. All it takes is hosting a meeting which may be scheduled twice a year, and then establishing a means to maintain the communication, such as electronic mail or telephone calls.

I credit much of the innovation and prosperity of Office Pride to the brainstorming and accountability sessions provided by my peer group.

Plans fail for lack of

counsel, but with many

advisers they succeed.

Proverbs 15:22

Chapter Thirty
Listen to the Right People

Did you ever look back on a decision and say to yourself "I should have followed my gut-feeling?" Why would you make a decision if you knew that it was not the right one? There is more than one way this can happen. As unlikely as it may seem, you most probably failed to acknowledge that you knew the right choice all along. You ignored your instincts. Another possibility is that you listened to the wrong people. We all have our true and trusted advisors, both in business and in other aspects of our lives. These may be our managers, our spouse, our pastor, our friends or mentors. Whoever they are, we regularly consult them on a variety of issues. Every now and then, however, we hesitate to go to them for advice. We fear they'll say what we don't want to hear. Ignoring their voice may lead to disaster.

I have learned that whenever I have an idea or decision that I do not wish to share with my trusted advisors, to walk away. I already know it is the wrong choice if I find myself desiring to hide it.

The Bible provides a great story of what can happen when we avoid trusted advisors and turn to just anyone who will agree with whatever we want to do. (I call these "YES men") Here's the story.

King Ahab learned his lesson the hard way (1 Kings 22: 1-38). After three years of peace between Syria and Israel, Ahab, King of Israel, had an urge to claim Ramoth-Gilead for his realm. King Ahab called his prophets, about four hundred of them, who agreed in unison to the success of the proposed campaign. One man, the prophet

Micaiah, had not yet been called. King Ahab knew him to be honest and truthful, but it frustrated him that Micaiah would never say what the King wanted to hear. Micaiah was reluctantly called and, as King Ahab had feared, prophesized that the King would be killed and his defeated people would return home without their leader.

King Ahab asked Micaiah how it could be possible that four hundred prophets would say one thing, and he would still insist on the opposite? Micaiah simply replied that a lying spirit had been put in the mouths of all these men, to entice the King to go up and fall at Ramoth-Gilead. King Ahab had Micaiah sent to prison and went to battle anyway. Bad call. He must have had some doubt in his heart, because he decided to shed his kingly robes and disguise himself as a soldier. In the thick of the fight, a rogue arrow pierced his armor and dealt him a slow and painful death. As predicted by Micaiah, at sunset a cry went through the army - to disperse and return home.

We should learn from King Ahab's mistake! Seek advice from those who have knowledge of your situation and who have access to Godly wisdom. Listen to them even when they tell you what you don't want to hear. Though you may not be risking life and kingdom, your reputation and integrity could be at stake.

Chapter Thirty-one
Consider What is Eternally Significant

There is no such thing as a Christian business. I know people mean well when they say they own a Christian business, but it is just not possible. A business is a thing of this world. It doesn't go to Heaven, it has no soul and it doesn't qualify for redemption. This is different than saying a business is owned and operated by Christians. In fact, how we go about and operate our business can have eternal significance. More than this, it is how you use your business to touch people's lives that you elevate your work to an eternally significant plane. Your path continuously crosses with employees, vendors, customers and colleagues. Your reach extends even further, often including their families and friends.

I remember this particularly gifted sales representative in charge of our account. His company provided some of our cleaning equipment and we were rapidly growing into one of their main customers. Sam was personable, humorous and very much alive. It was a pleasure to see him when he came over weekly to visit our account. We often talked over a cup of coffee. He was always interested in my faith and in the role it played in my business life. I shared with Sam, as I am doing with you in this book, my experience starting a business and the times God's power had been manifested in the business. I invited Sam to a businessmen's outreach being held by the local CBMC group. It was there that Sam gave his life to Jesus Christ.

One day, shortly after, a lady approached me and thanked me profusely for helping her son.

This was Sam's mom. She was deeply spiritual and it had pained her to see that Sam had rejected any mention of her faith. Sam had often expressed to her his discontentment with God, and how he didn't see any practical application for a life of worship. Now, all that had changed. Sam was a new man with a purpose.

God will open doors. Sam calling on me that first time was one of those divine appointments. I am grateful God allowed me the privilege of being used in an eternally significant way. And He did it through the business.

God orchestrates divine appointments for us. Make sure you show up when He expects you to. The next person you see at a business meeting could be one for whom God has chosen you to be His witness. These "chance" meetings happen all the time. God, through the Holy Spirit, is behind it all.

It is so easy to get self-absorbed with our own cares. We forget to pray for God to show us in what way He is going to use our business, the one with which He has blessed us, for His divine purposes. Please know that God will act through you, regardless of whether your business is succeeding or failing. In fact, believers who are "going out of business" are carefully watched by non-believers as a point of reference. I hope this is not your case, but if it is, show the world the peace, joy and absolute sustaining love of Christ. Be ready for your meeting. This is the moment of truth, where the rubber meets the road.

Are you up to the challenge?

Chapter Thirty-two
Share Your Story

Many people are very shy and would never speak in public, not even attempt it. Unfortunately, this is often used as an excuse not to share God's grace in their lives. Somehow, it occurs to me that Satan gives them this "reason" to keep them from sharing their faith with other people. My experience has been that the words of a quiet, seldom outspoken person, are often the most respected.

All believers have a story worth telling. Next

time you have an opportunity to share, commit to it. The rest will take care of itself. Here is how:

First, pray that God will impart His message through you.

Second, prepare notes on what you would like to say. Think of all the ways that God has worked in your life and how this has carried over to your business. It is likely that if you have been invited to speak, there are people who are already interested in what you have to say.

Third, practice as often as you can.

Finally, put your trust in the Lord to get you through the message and Go! You can open your speech by sharing with your audience how the thought of speaking in public used to terrify you and how you have placed your confidence in God to guide you through it. You can follow by saying how His work is fully evident in the mere fact that you are standing there, speaking to them!

Think of the blind man. (John 9:25) He simply did not know how or why Jesus had given him back his sight. All he knew were three simple facts: he was blind, Jesus anointed his eyes, and

120

now he could see. And this is what he said to all who were willing to hear.

Follow the example of the blind man and be a witness to God's glory. You will not only reach out to someone who is thirsty for His knowledge, but you will also build your own confidence, as you are once again reminded of the many miracles that God has worked in your life.

I have found great reward in sharing my personal testimony. It reminds me of God's wonderful grace in my life. As a business owner, I often tell people my two greatest threats rhythm: EGO and CASH FLOW. My ego is checked each time I share or repeat my testimony as I am reminded to give God the glory for the success we have had at Office Pride.

Chapter Thirty-three
Forgive Those Who Wrong You

For the first time in my life, I was looking at a notice informing us that the company owned by Jack, one of our long-standing customers, had filed for bankruptcy, leaving an unpaid invoice hanging in the void. The amount of money owed to us was significant at the time, and my stomach tightened thinking of the sacrifices I would have to make to compensate for this shortfall. Such was my frame of mind when I scheduled a meeting with Jack, to see if I could persuade him to pay us.

He explained that the FAA had delayed approval of one of his new products. His business had invested all its capital in research and development for this product, but until the FAA gave the go ahead, he could neither manufacture nor sell it.

Although I felt sorry for him, I couldn't help thinking that he should have planned for such a scenario. Since government approval was an integral part of the product he was launching, an administrative delay could hardly be called an "unforeseen circumstance." He pleaded with me, as he had done with his other vendors, to stick with him and see this crisis through. All I could think about was my pending invoice, so I decided to go along with Jack in the hope of someday getting it paid.

Three months later, Jack called me to come out and get our cleaning equipment because his business was closing. As I was carrying out the last of the items, I caught a glimpse of Jack through the half-open door to his office. He was the image of defeat. Here was a man with no hope, a life devoid of faith. I left him sitting there in the darkness, hoping that I would never have to go through something like that. There was no room in my heart for compassion, it was too cold with resentment for this man and his unpaid promise.

In retrospect, what I see is a missed opportunity. I could have been light, I could have been salt. I was neither. Instead of showing a sullen stone face, like all the other creditors, I could have been a good witness and allowed Jack to feel the peace of Christ working through me. His heart might have opened, willing to learn more about this wonderful Lord and Savior who granted me such peace. Jack could have learned about all the times Office Pride would have failed if it hadn't been saved through God's intervention. How different our last meeting would have been if I had only extended a friendly hand to Jack to say: "I forgive you for the money you owe us. God will provide in some other way, as He will provide for you if you let Him into your life."

Here is my advice to you: for all those who have wronged you, you need to forgive and move on. To the customer who didn't hire your services and the employee who cheated you - offer them your forgiveness, and be blessed. You cannot plow straight if you are looking backwards (Luke 9:62). God is a God of forwardness. You need to look directly ahead towards your vision to keep your purpose strong. No good will ever come from holding on to your grudges.

Jesus replied, "No one who puts his hand to the plow and looks back is fit for service in the kingdom of God."

Luke 9:62 (NIV)

Chapter Thirty-four
Give Thanks

I am getting some writing done on a flight back home after a long business trip. Nine days is the longest I have ever been away from my wife and kids. My thoughts are centered on how exhausting this trip has been. I can't wait to get home. The captain announces that air traffic control has directed our flight to a holding pattern, causing a delay in our arrival. I reach over to my briefcase to check how much time I have before my connecting flight. I make eye contact with another passenger two seats over from me checking the same thing, we give each other a resigned smile. I had noticed this young lady before but since it was obvious she was not feeling well, I hadn't attempted to start a conversation.

"Are you missing your connection?" she asks.

"I may still make it. I am really anxious to get back home to my family," I reply.

"I know what you mean!" she says softly. "I have been away for 28 days. My husband and my seven-month-old little girl couldn't come with me. I miss them so much! My name is Marie."

The conversation went on to the usual polite small talk between tired fellow travelers. After a while, Marie started telling me about the reason for her trip. In my self-centered preoccupation, I had almost failed to realize that I was in the presence of genuine human suffering. Marie had leukemia. Her doctors had discovered this when she gave birth to her daughter. She was on her way back from a trip to receive treatment in a specialized hospital. It had been a harrowing experience. Her husband had stayed behind because they couldn't afford to miss a paycheck.

Making ends meet was getting harder with her not working. Her illness had forced her to take a year off her job as a first-grade teacher, but she promised the school that she would be back next year. She absently whispered, "I hope I'll be able to keep that promise."

I asked her if she was a believer, and was relieved to hear her tell me about her faith. I told her I would pray for her as she comes to mind.

This sobering encounter helped me to take stock of the abundant blessings in my life. Here I was, internally whining about a nine-day business trip, while I had good health, a wonderful family, a thriving business - more blessings than I could possibly deserve.

Every time we allow ourselves to get caught up in our own worldly concerns, we miss God's splendid creation and blessings around us.

This may be a good time for you to stop reading and take stock of your many blessings. Marie's circumstances sure helped me put the toil of owning a business into proper perspective.

Be joyful always; pray continually, give thanks in all circumstances, for this is God's will for you in Christ Jesus.

I Thessalonians 5:16-18

(NIV)

Chapter Thirty-five
Weather the Storm

Some of the best insight on overcoming adversity comes from Acts 27:9-29. Paul is on his way to Rome as a prisoner. The Centurion Julius escorted him on board the ship that would carry him to his destination. The trip was taking longer than expected. The winds had not been favorable. The majority on board wanted to press on, to round Crete and reach the port of Phoenix, where they could winter. Paul, a Godly man, wisely advised against it, recommending they remain in

Fair Havens. He tried to reason that the weather that time of year made the sailing conditions highly dangerous. But Julius listened to the Captain and the owner of the ship instead, so they continued, reasoning that he liked the Captain's advice because Phoenix was a much better place to hang out for the winter.

Once they put out to sea, just as Paul had predicted, a fierce northeasterly wind whipped them dangerously off their plotted course. The violent storm churned them around, giving no signs of abating. They tossed overboard all their cargo and even the ships vital equipment and sailing tackle. All hope of being saved was abandoned.

And then Paul spoke again. You might have expected a good "I told you so" speech. Instead, Paul brought good news. He had been visited by an Angel of God. The messenger told him not to be afraid, that he would appear before the Caesar, and the entire crew would survive. Paul urged the defeated crew to have faith, instructed them to eat in order to keep their strength, and to stick together, in order to be saved. This time they listened to Paul. On the fourteenth day, they sighted land, and even though the ship was destroyed, they made it to safety on the island of Malta.

As I reflect on this passage it occurs to me that many times we get into the thick of a storm by our own doing. We make hasty decisions by listening to the majority, or to the wrong experts, because they say what we want to hear. We rely heavily on circumstances without weighing the consequences.

The moral of this story may sound like the same as that of King Ahab in an earlier chapter. It bears repeating as I have seen many businesses fail because the owner surrounded himself or herself with advisors and employees who would never challenge any decisions she made. This false sense of confidence is impending doom. It is critical to teach and encourage our team members to respectfully challenge us when it is for the good of the company. And be open to the possibility that they may have a better idea or understanding of a situation than we do.

Back to the story. Storms affect our lives in

many ways - we get lost, we suffer losses, we despair. Paul shows us three anchors to help us weather any storm.

The first one is to have God's *presence* in our life, which Paul had received and which is revealed through his heart and in the visit from an Angel.

Second, there is the *plan* that God has for our lives, as it was Paul's purpose to meet the Caesar. It was also his purpose to minister to the men on the ship. By the time they left Malta they were listening to Paul and, most likely, believing in his God.

The third anchor is God's *promise* - Paul had faith that everything would happen exactly as he had been told.

Next time you are adrift and about to give up hope, hold on to God's presence, plan and promise, until you reach your own island of safety. Once you reach your safety zone, don't let go of the anchors. They work awesomely during the good times too!

Commit to the Lord whatever you do, and your plans will succeed.

Proverbs 16:3 (NIV)

Chapter Thirty-six
Enjoy Your Family

How can I describe in mere words the joy that my family brings to my heart? Just close your eyes and go back for a moment to the time when you were at your absolute happiest. That is how I feel when my wife and I play a board game with our children or while saying prayers with them at bedtime. Any trouble I had during the day just melts away in an instant and I get renewed inspiration to keep going.

Now, I need to get personal with you for a

minute and what I am about to say could hurt. In all my life, I have never heard anyone say they wished they would have spent <u>less</u> time with their kids. I will even go a step farther and say that an entrepreneur who has grown a magnificent business; but, destroyed his or her family in the "PROCESS", is not a success at all.

What an awesome privilege it is to be a parent.

Families come in many shapes. Whether two-parent, single-parent, adoptive, foster or otherwise; families provide their unique challenges and satisfactions. Children in our society are often viewed as a liability. You can even get a tax deduction for having kids! In case you are either planning to start a family or you already have one and you are wondering how to combine work and home, please read Psalm 127. I could write an entire book on the power of this message. "Sons are a heritage from the Lord, Children a reward from Him." (Psalm 127:3 NIV). You will find that there are times when you need to keep a strong focus to remember that your children are a reward from God.

I have talked to a number of people who have admitted that they got so focused on their business that they lost sight of their personal lives and their families eventually broke down. On the opposite side of the coin, I have talked to frustrated business people who are trying to juggle business and family life. If you ask me, they are just trying too hard to do everything themselves. We need to let the Lord into our lives and let him do the building, both in our family as well as in our business. Why do we deny ourselves His magnificent power and keep banging our heads against walls of our own doing?

Many people respond that this is easier said than done. I stand on Proverbs 16:3, "Commit to the Lord whatever you do, and your plans will succeed." (NIV) What an awesome verse to build a family and a business on. Why will we succeed if we do this? Well, in the King James Version, this verse in the Bible tells us, "our thoughts will be established." Can you imagine committing every personal and business decision to God and then having Him give you the thoughts you need to make the right decision. WOW!

I am a firm believer (and living proof) that you can have it all, a thriving business and a loving family. It is the very presence of God in my own life that has enabled me to be one of those so fortunate.

Unless the Lord builds the house, its builders labor in vain. Unless the Lord watches over the city, the watchmen stand guard in vain.

Psalm 127:1 (NIV)

Chapter Thirty-seven
Enjoy Going to Work

I wish to share with you more words from Richard Sickels, whose mentorship has meant so much to me and has provided such rich and generous guidance. Here is what Richard shared with me recently over lunch, when I asked him how he became involved in sales: "I started as a volunteer!" he chuckled (referring to when he was the General Manager of a Christian radio broadcasting station). "At the time, I owned an electrical service business. I used to listen to the Christian station, and decided to stop by and tell them how much I enjoyed their programming.

The General Manager greeted me on the defensive, since listeners usually stop by in person only to complain about something. I said I was just there to thank him, because his station was a blessing to me. I asked him if there was anything I could do for them. He paused for a minute and said that maybe I could pray for the radio station Love 98.3FM, listen to them, and <u>tell people about them</u>. I said I would do that. And I did! I took every Friday afternoon off and visited local establishments. I asked them what they were listening to, and if they would consider trying this station. I praised their beautiful music and family oriented programming. Some of them had never heard of the station.

One day I visited a printing business, and the owner said he liked the programming so much that he would like to advertise on it. I explained that I didn't work at the station and was just a volunteer, but that I would convey his message to the General Manager. When I did, the General Manager gingerly handed me a media kit and asked me if I would mind taking it back to the printer since he had an important meeting he couldn't miss. I went back to the printer, who signed the contract and wrote me a check for $1,500 on the spot. The General Manager was highly amused and forced me into accepting a commission for the sale."

"After a while," Richard continued, "I was spending so much time promoting radio that my brother, who worked for me in my electrical business, decided to approach me with a proposal. Since I was obviously enjoying my work for the radio station, resulting in my brother having to do most of the work in our business, would I consider selling the business to him? I named the highest price I could dream of. Not long after, my brother accepted the offer and the deal was closed. I went back to the radio station and told the General Manager that I had just become a full-time volunteer! He was uneasy at first because he could not pay me a salary. I was not concerned and I never looked back. For over 20 years, I loved my job every single day."

With genuine sincerity, Richard said, "I am saddened when people tell me that they don't enjoy what they do. Ultimate success is found in being what God created us to be. When all is said and done, God will not congratulate us for selling lots of advertising, or having a great number of franchisees. He will ask us what we did with what He gave us. And I will be able to say to Him that, although I failed in many ways, I loved people and when I saw a need, I tried to give.

I have received many blessings through my work at the radio station. The key that opened this door for me was to ask the General Manager, on that first meeting, what I could do to help. As you begin to help people, guess what happens? God's blessings will overtake you. We miss the point when we become self-focused, when we seek to see only what is in it for us. It is only when we become God-focused that we fulfill our purpose." I agreed with Richard and mentioned the example we find in Mathew 14:28-31. "Exactly!" he said with enthusiasm "remember that as long as Peter kept his eyes focused on Jesus, he was able to walk on water, even during a fierce storm. As soon as he became concerned about his circumstances, doubt entered his heart and he began to sink. In the same way, as long as we remain focused on the purpose that God created us for, we will be blessed and doors will open." (II Cor 9:8-9)

Richard continued, "Can you think of a more focused person than Jesus? He was the ultimate servant. Jesus was Lord, yet he humbled himself, as on the occasion when he washed the feet of his disciples. He even washed the feet of his betrayer. Jesus, through his actions, showed a pattern, for us to get the message: Love God and love one another. It is not only His teaching but His principles we see at work today. We can observe them at work even in Fortune 500 companies.

There was a survey conducted to identify the main cause of loss of goodwill from customers. Results revealed that neither price, location, product specifications, nor changes in customers needs drove their rejection. Do you know what the main complaint was? Customers did not feel that the company cared about them. Keep that in mind when you deal with your customers. Call them regularly, ask them what they need. Help people, serve them (even when they spite you or when they are mean to you). Did Jesus refuse to wash Judas' feet, even knowing that he would betray Him? Follow His lead. Make sure your love for your clients is unconditional. To love people, is to love God."

"One of the highest compliments I have ever received," Richard explained, "came from one of the owners of the radio station. This gentleman, who owned many radio stations, came to me and told me that I was the best radio sales person he knew. This compliment was enhanced by the fact that he didn't follow my same faith, he was Jewish. Do you know why I am so successful at sales? I help people. I ask them what they need, and how I can serve them. I am not there to sell them something. I evaluate their needs. If I believe that I can help, then I ask them for permission to make a presentation. You always need to ask! I tell them about my product, and transfer my enthusiasm and sincerity in its qualities. I ask them if promoting their business is important to them. I ask them what value they would place on it. And many times, I get to serve them. Many times they don't need radio advertising, so I help them in other ways. Sometimes just pointing them in the right direction makes a difference in their lives. I have made many friends, and I have also seen many broken lives."

Richard continues, "My purpose is to be a blessing to other people. A business owner's son approached me ten or fifteen years after I had visited his father, to ask me for advice. He said his father had told him that I was a trustworthy man, because I hadn't tried to sell him something he didn't need. That means more to me than just obsessing about closing the deal. And you know what else is interesting? The more you give, the more blessings you receive. Once in this very restaurant, as I prepared to pray before my meal, I asked the lady serving my table if there was anything she would like me to pray for. She immediately said yes, her husband had been arrested the day before, and she had four babies to take care of and very little income. I prayed for her. A few months later I ran into her coming out of the restaurant with her husband. She thanked me for my prayers. She said they were going to church as a family now, he was a good husband, and her babies were all fine. She remembered I was the guy from the Christian radio, and said she would talk to her boss to buy some advertising. This was just icing on the cake!" Richard beamed with joy, remembering this family. "As we learn from 2 Corinthians 9:6, if we sow little we shall reap little, but if we sow generously, we will reap bountifully. Let me tell you, I have reaped more than I could have ever possibly imagined."

Richard speaks with the conviction of personal experience. I could listen to him for hours. Whenever I talk to Richard, I feel my faith renewed. My heart is warm with enthusiasm. I have been truly blessed with his friendship. If you do not have a mentor, begin to pray that God will bring one into your life.

Chapter Thirty-eight
Define Success Correctly

Once you have given yourself to your work, the line that defines success becomes so fine that it is hard to tell when you've actually crossed it. In my experience, success is better defined by the way you travel, rather than the destination. Success is often mistaken with fame, although fame is rarely permanent.

Let me give you one example that comes to mind. When I was working on my MBA, I sat next to an older gentleman in one of my classes. His name was Mr. Johnson and I could tell from small talk that he had tremendous experience when it came to business. In fact, for several weeks I wondered why he was even in school. I was 22 years old at the time and he must have been over 50. As it became time to work on the final class research project, the professor told us to find a classmate with whom to partner. Mr. Johnson and I decided to work together as a team. We had to meet twice a week for the last three weeks and during that time I learned a lot about how to define success.

I asked Mr. Johnson about his career and why he had returned to school after all these years. He explained to me that he had started his own computer service business at the early age of 30. Initially the service he offered (sending a computer programmer to your office and charging by the hour) was a bit ahead of its time, but later became far from unique. During the 1980s, the competition was tough, and Mr. Johnson soon found that, with all the interest in the industry, the time was right to take the company public. He did this in

1990 and found himself sitting on over $50 million in stock.

His dream had come true. He was rich and famous. His high school actually recognized him with the Most Successful Alumnus of the Decade Award. He bought a big house, a boat and a vacation condo. He was envied by many peers.

I had remembered him telling me that he had three kids, so I asked him how his wife and kids liked the big life. That was when, his tone of voice changed dramatically, and he looked away and said, "That's where I lost out." As I opened my mouth to ask him for more detail, he continued, "In the world's eye, I was a big success. I had the money, I was involved in the community, but I was not there for my wife and the kids when they needed me most. When I missed our youngest son's high school graduation to attend a charity event hosted by one of our largest customers, my wife finally gave up on me. She divorced me and rather than try to get half of what I had, she told me I could keep it all."

"For the first time in my life, I felt like a failure, and worst yet, a failure at something that really mattered. My wife was gone. My kids were grown and I really didn't know them." When I asked him what happened to his business, he remarked very uncaringly, "In the second quarter of 1992, with competition at an all-time high, we missed our earnings projection. Wall Street is not a forgiving place. Stock values dropped, employees jumped ship, and I was replaced as President by my very own Board of Directors. I ended up losing most of my assets, but kept enough to retire and live a comfortable life." To most, Mr. Johnson's roller coaster had one exhilarating up and one crushing down. And that was it. Mr. Johnson's success came and went in the eyes of the world.

Once he hit the wall and had no family, Mr. Johnson turned to the one friendship that was <u>not</u> created as a result of his success. It was his younger brother, Joseph. Joseph shared with Mr. Johnson that true success has a deeper, more permanent nature. This type of success is the one that comes with doing what God has created us for, not with what the world judges us by.

God has given each of us a special purpose. For some it may be to become the leader of a business. For others it may mean being Godly spouses or parents. Ultimately the measure of success is not indicated by arbitrary public or media perception, but through the position in life that we have attained in harmony with God's purpose. Joseph led his brother into a relationship with Jesus Christ that day.

Four days later, Mr. Johnson was on a plane to Houston to see his ex-wife and beg for her forgiveness. She forgave, they re-married and he has been reunited with his kids. Now, he says he is pursuing the one thing he always wanted to do and that was be a teacher. His wife is the principal of a small private school and he plans to join her there. He stayed out of that profession earlier in life, because, "there was no money in it". But now purpose is more important to him than money and he has been called to go to the classroom. He is getting his Master's Degree in Education and was taking this business class as an elective.

Do not allow the world's definition of success to discourage you. You may be more successful than you give yourself credit for, if you only measure your success, not by the world's standards, but by God's purpose for you. In my experience, when the "PROCESS" of owning a business gets rocky or seemingly unsuccessful, I turn to God for clarity of purpose in my life. Without fail, the current business issues are put in proper perspective and I move forward with renewed peace and vision.

Therefore, since we are surrounded by such a great cloud of witnesses, let us throw off everything that hinders and the sin that so easily entangles, and let us run with perseverance the race marked out for us.

Hebrews 12:1 (NIV)

155

Chapter Thirty-nine
Establish the Right Foundation

I saved this chapter for last, because I not only wanted this book to reflect my experiences in business, but also to share with you how I arrived at my personal relationship with Jesus Christ.

I grew up in Tennessee, as part of a loving family. We attended church every Sunday, and at the age of eleven I was baptized, along with my younger brother. I went on to college and all along had this urgent drive to succeed. I wanted to excel in academics and sports, and had a goal to become the "Big Man On Campus."

It goes without saying that once I became a businessman, competitiveness remained at the center of my field of vision. I equated being happy with making a lot of money and buying nice things. After I moved to Indiana, I had a group of friends with whom I played basketball, and one of the guys, Keith Tyner, invited me to a CBMC outreach meeting for local businessmen. As the speaker at this meeting shared his story, my heart went out to him. He had experienced unspeakable tragedy. Three of his four children had died as a result of illness or injury. The first thought that came through my mind was, "How does he do it? What gives him the strength to be standing here today talking to us?" As if on cue, this man said that the only thing that had carried him through it all was his relationship with Jesus Christ.

Through the foundations and principles he had learned from the scriptures he was able to focus on God instead of on his heartbreaking circumstances. After that day, a growing conviction gradually took shape in my heart. I needed a relationship with Jesus Christ. A personal relationship.

Remember how I said that I wanted to succeed? Well, that includes going to Heaven when I die. I had always assumed I would go to Heaven, because I was an overall good person and had even been baptized as a kid. But, just in case, I started checking to make sure. I became an academic and applied myself to the study of scripture. On Wednesday mornings I joined a group of businessmen for Bible study. On one particular day the subject was going to be "baptism". This was my chance to confirm if I was going to Heaven or not. During the meeting, a man rose and declared: "Baptism alone won't save you, it will only send you to hell soaking wet!" The whole room erupted in laughter. Except I wasn't laughing at all. My salvation was hanging precariously on my baptism, and I had just heard that it wasn't good enough.

Even though I had tried to be a good Christian, and I was pretty sure that my good side outweighed my not-so-good one, my confidence sank. And the more I learned, the more I realized that the only way to salvation was through a personal relationship with Jesus. I read Romans 3:23 "...for all have sinned and fall short of the glory of God...." I didn't have a problem with that, I knew I was a sinner. I haven't met a single person who would say that they have never committed a sin.

But I was haunted by Romans 6:23 "For the wages of sin is death, but the gift of God is eternal life in Christ Jesus our Lord." The price we pay for sin is death, meaning eternal separation from God, in hell. I certainly did not want to pay for my sins by being separated from God. And then the alternative became clear to me in Acts 3:19 "Repent, then, and turn to God, so that your sins may be wiped out, that times of refreshing may come from the Lord." We have a choice! We can repent. It became even clearer in Romans 10:9-10 "That if you confess with your mouth, 'Jesus is Lord' and believe in your heart that God raised him from the dead, you will be saved. For it is with your heart that you believe and are justified, and it is with your mouth that you confess and are saved."

At this point I was beginning to see the true way to salvation. I learned that we have a choice, if we want to receive Jesus Christ as our Lord and Savior, to allow the payment that He made for us on the cross to be applied to our account. I knew that was what I wanted; to be able to spend eternity in Heaven - with God.

And then came October 15th, 1989. I was twenty-four. There was nothing special going on, except that I had been asked by the singles' group I belonged to in church, to share my testimony. I was an extrovert and had no problem addressing the crowd of about 250 people that night. I talked about what God was doing in my life, and I could hear the preacher punctuate my speech with a resounding "Amen" here and there. All my friends came up to congratulate me. That was a good sign. And yet, on my way home, my heart was still pounding, and I was miserably confused. It was then that I admitted the following to myself: It didn't matter if the pastor or my friends thought I was going to Heaven. It is only God's opinion that counts. I realized I had never truly invited Jesus into my life. When I reached home that night I got down on my knees, and said my simplest and most honest prayer:

"Dear Lord, I gave my testimony tonight, and I don't really know if I even have a testimony. I don't know for sure if I have a relationship with Jesus Christ. But, right now, for the record, I want to pray and ask Jesus to enter my life, to be my Lord and Savior. If you will help me understand what your will is for my life, I'll do my best to live it. Thank you. Amen."

I can't say that I heard any bells ringing or saw any fireworks go off. I did feel a sense of relief though, as if a weight had been taken off my shoulders. The only way I can explain it is that I felt I was no longer in charge of my own eternal life, God was, so I was now in the hands of the expert. God is in the business of eternal life, He can handle it, I can't. (If you are a non-believer or still have doubts in your heart, I invite you to say this simple prayer. It is life changing.)

I also decided to share with God my one nagging doubt. What if after living this Christian life there is not such a place as Heaven? Is it all a waste? Within two weeks I had my answer. The man who had stood at the Bible study meeting to declare that baptism alone wasn't enough, had died in his sleep. I never liked funerals, so as I approached his son to express my condolences. I was nervously trying to find the appropriate words to make him feel better, to ease his grief. And then I noticed the most extraordinary thing. There was joy in the people attending the funeral. They were celebrating this man who had lived a good life and had led others to God. Here was a man that would hear Jesus say "Well done, my good and faithful servant!" I no longer had any doubts. This man had gone to heaven. This was confirmed by the joy that filled the hearts of the people he left behind.

So I take this opportunity to say here to all those who know me: rejoice at my funeral! No need to worry about Todd Hopkins. I have a relationship with Jesus Christ, and I am going to Heaven!

God has done wonderful things in my life. He

healed my marriage and I now have a truly loving relationship with my wife. He brought my mentor into my life, at the time when I most needed his support. He has blessed me with three wonderful children and in so many other ways, more than I can express. The more I experience God and trust Him, the easier it is for me to lean on Him when I am challenged by difficulties. My goal is to focus on God, and rise over my circumstances. I couldn't imagine operating a business or surviving as an entrepreneur without having God in the center of it. I know now that there is but one true success: our success in God's eyes.

I sincerely hope that you enjoyed reading this book as much as I enjoyed writing it, and that you found here some useful insight that will help you along your chosen journey. May you always look with hope on the path that lies ahead. Many blessings.

For God so loved the world

that he gave his one and

only Son, that whoever

believes in him shall not

perish but have eternal life.

John 3:16 (NIV)

Acknowledgements

I would like to give a special thanks to the following:

Michelle, my wife, for encouraging me to finally sit down and write this book and for living out the entire experience with me.

James, Sam and Matt for being the greatest sons a dad could ever want.

Richard Sickels, Eldon Kibbey, Troy Hopkins, Daniel Hooper, Karen Tomasovic, Andrew Palmer, Mark Wages, Blake Clements, John McBeath, Pastor Rick Henry, Verne Harnish and Stan

Corfman for providing valuable feedback and edits for this book.

Sylvia Edwards Davis for her creative help and keeping me to a schedule.

Doug Jolly for the cover design.

Pastor Gary Stump for all the encouragement and advice in the early years. Pastor Randy Maynard for your loving kindness to me and my family. Pastor John Spencer for teaching the WORD faithfully.

Teresa McClure, Dr. Linda Frechette and Tom Helmbock for believing in me and providing encouragement at just the right time.

My mom and dad, James and Sheila Hopkins, for always believing in me and supporting me in everything.

The Office Pride corporate staff, employees and franchise owners who have taught me so much and have helped make Office Pride what it is today.

Office Pride customers, vendors and business associates for believing in Office Pride and contributing greatly to our team's image, expertise and success.

My Young Entrepreneur's Organization forum members who challenged me and provided great insight when I needed it most.

My CBMC brothers, who have prayed for me diligently over the years and who have been the source of great and Godly wisdom.

Keith Tyner, Bill Balbach, Terry Lingner, Ted Grossnickle and the others who have invested in the vision of Office Pride and hold me accountable to being a good steward.

Jesus Christ who died on the cross for me and who has provided a purpose for my life.

These are great books that I recommend you read:

Holy Bible

The E Myth Revisited by Michael E. Gerber

Mastering the Rockefeller Habits by Verne Harnish

Leadership and Self-Deception by The Arbinger Institute

The Five Temptations of a CEO by Patrick Lencioni

How To Become A Great Boss by Jeffrey J. Fox

Rich Dad, Poor Dad by Robert T. Kiyosaki

Good To Great by Jim Collins

Commercial Cleaning Services

The mission of Office Pride Commercial Cleaning Services is to honor and glorify God by building mutually beneficial relationships with customers, employees, vendors, and franchise owners and fulfilling our promise of providing top quality janitorial services through men and women committed to honesty, integrity and hard work.

Commercial Cleaning Services

Franchise and Area Development opportunities available.

For more information on Office Pride Commercial Cleaning
Services contact us at:

Office Pride
170 North Jackson Street
Franklin, IN 46131
Phone (317) 738-9280
Fax: (317) 738-5299

Or visit us at www.officepride.com

You may contact Todd Hopkins directly
at 317-738-9280
or by email to todd@officepride.com

170